S

us

UP Date

# DAD from a
# Distance

## HOW NON-CUSTODIAL FATHERS CAN STILL BE FANTASTIC DADS

To Justin,
All the best!

# GREG GRAY

## This book is dedicated to:

My Dad, the late Thomas Gray, Jr.,
who was excellence personified and who,
through the power of his example, taught me what it
really means to be a  great Dad.

My Mom, Valeria Gray,
whose love, strength, selflessness, and courage
have always been the solid foundation for our family
and the glue that holds us together.

My daughter Danielle,
who was the first person to "hire" me
as a Dad and has graciously kept me on the job, and whose
wit and passion for life  inspire me every day.

My stepdaughters, Semi and Aleecia,
who have lovingly allowed me be a part of their lives, and
are my constant reminder that one size  does not fit all
when it comes to loving those close to you.

And my to wife Melodie,
who is my compass in the midst of the storm,
and whose love, generosity, integrity, and wisdom
continue to make me a better man.

Three of my favorite words:

"That's my Dad!"

# Foreword
## by the Author's Daughter

When my Dad asked me to write the foreword for "Dad from a Distance", I was excited and nervous all at the same time. I also didn't really know why he chose me to write it, so I asked, and he said "When it comes to having someone introduce me as an author on a book on being a Dad, no one in the world is more credible than you". That totally sums up who my Dad is. He cares deeply about being a great Dad and about every man being a great Dad. That he has been such a wonderful Dad to me "from a distance" is almost a secondary consideration because of the wonderful relationship we have.

Since he gave me this task, I have written the beginning of this foreword seemingly a million times, not because I couldn't find the right words to say, but because what my Dad means to me and what he has done for me cannot easily be put into words.

You should know that while my parents divorced when I was six years old, I find it striking that I can recall absolutely no time that my dad was absent in my life. He always made me feel that I would be his priority and his "little princess" forever.

Whether it was all the 'daddy magic' (his magical healing power) that he gave me when I hurt myself on the playground or when I didn't get picked to be on the varsity team or even when I thought that Division I Women's Basketball was the hardest thing in my life, he was always there. My Dad answered my calls whenever I needed to talk to him (sometimes about absolutely nothing) over lunch and often from hundreds of miles away. He would send me postcards from every part of the country that he had been in, and at every opportunity, he would tickle me until I couldn't breathe. My every memory is filled with a Dad who was there.

Now I know that no one is perfect, and as you get older, as I am now a college graduate, you see the flaws in people and you realize that everyone is 'human'. And believe me, my Dad knows he doesn't know it all, mainly because I've reminded him of that on occasion. That was evident when I was shuttled over to my mom's house when I 'became a woman' or when I wanted to talk about how dumb boys are. And yes, I would also hate when he would seemingly butt in to all of the problems I was having with any coaches or teachers, and just like any other young teen-ager, I was embarrassed that he was always around or that he made so much noise during my games, but when I look back over it all, he was always there. Even with his flaws, I have never seen my Dad as a regular man; I've always seen him as my superhero.

What is also telling is that not only was my Dad my hero, he became an 'adopted' Dad for many of my friends who didn't have their fathers actively involved in their lives and that made me appreciate him all that much more. I was, and still am, proud to share him with others because he molded their ideas of what a good Dad really was, and proved to them that good men, and good Dads actually do exist. Do you feel bad for my future husband yet? (smile)

So as you read this book about being a good "Dad from a Distance", know that this is from a man that has done it and knows what he is talking about. And know that, although you may become a better Dad with my Dad's help, I'm not sure you will ever be a better Daddy than mine (come on, he's my superhero). But I do know that what he writes about in this book is real, that it works, and that it comes straight from his heart.

Finally, it would be perfectly understandable for you to think I am telling you all this just to help him with his book. You may even think that he has written it for me to make it seem more appealing, but for some reason, I believe, in my heart, you will feel the love in my words and know that I'm just telling you how I feel about the number one man in my life.

Simply put, my Dad has always been there for me and always will be. Don't you want your son or daughter to say the same?

Danielle Gray

# Table of Contents

# Dad from a Distance
# Introduction

If you are reading this, either you've recently found yourself in the role of a non-custodial Father, have been in that role for some time, or anticipate being in that role soon, or you know someone who is or will be in that role, and thought this book might be helpful.

Whatever the reason, let me begin by saying "Thank you".

Thank you for making the choice to dedicate or rededicate yourself to the important task of enhancing your very important relationship with your child or children.

If you aren't a Dad from a Distance, but know someone who is, thank you for your willingness to help him in this important life-long effort.

I want you to know that writing this book has been a labor of love that was inspired by some very serious realities.

First, I've grown weary of the constant drumbeat of news and opinion that have labeled so many non-custodial Fathers as bad Dads. I've grown weary of it not because in many cases it isn't true, but because it doesn't have to be the case.

Second, most parents know that there is no "how to" manual that comes with being a parent and that even parents in the most model nuclear families still often find themselves struggling with parenting skills. I find that this challenge is compounded when it comes to non-custodial Fathers.

For some non-custodial Fathers, it's no doubt true that their lack of involvement and participation in their child's lives is the result of a lack of **will**. For many others, however, I submit to you that it is also in great measure a lack of **skill** – of not knowing what to do, and how and when to do it.

When you couple these realities with the complex and sometimes difficult dynamics that often exist in the relationship between the non-custodial Father and the child or children's Mother, it seems for some Fathers that having a good relationship with their child/children is or can be just too steep and difficult a hill to climb.

Consequently, I wanted to provide a blueprint, if you will, of specific things non-custodial Fathers can think about and do to maximize the quality of the relationships they have with their children - **your** children.

Now to be clear, let me also be straightforward as to what this book is **not** about.

It is **not** about analyzing the sequence of events that led to you being a non-custodial Father. There is a very long list of potential candidates when it comes to the causes and/or circumstances that can lead you to being in this situation – far too many for me to attempt to discuss in this book. And besides, I'm not qualified to do so anyway.

It is **not** about affixing blame to any one party or helping you resolve relationship issues with your child's Mother. That's between the two of you. This book is about helping you enrich the relationship between you and your child.

It is **not** about trying to convince non-custodial Fathers that their children are important enough to put forth the effort I'll be suggesting in this book. My assumption is that if you're reading this book, your child being a priority in your life is a settled matter. In other words, this book is designed to enhance your "skill" set, not your "will" set. If your "will" set gets enhanced along the way, we'll count that as a bonus.

Why should you care what I have to say? Well, it's because this is not a theoretical undertaking for me. It's real life. I've been and still am "there".

I became a non-custodial parent through divorce when my daughter was 6 years old. Understanding that I would not wake up in the same house with her just down the hall was one of the most traumatic things I've ever experienced, and my having to tell her that this would be the case ripped through my very soul. It's a moment frozen in time that even more than two decades later, is still difficult for me to talk or think about and, on occasion, still haunts my dreams.

If you've been through this, you know exactly what I'm talking about.

To add to the "Distance", at the time I found myself in this new role, as part of my work, I traveled all over the country 40 plus weeks a year. So the distance between my daughter and I was not just magnified simply by a different address, but often by hundreds or thousands of miles.

All of this combined to make this new situation devastating and heartbreaking all at once. But at the same time, it lit a fire in me that burned hotter than the sun - a fire that inspired me to be more than just a non-custodial Father (that's just a legal status), but to maintain and build on my role as a "Dad". Along the way, I've made a lot of good choices and I've made a lot of mistakes. This book is in essence a compilation of what I have leaned and what I am learning as I continue my quest to be the best Dad I can possibly be.

In other words, my greatest inspiration for writing and sharing this book comes from the deep love I have for my "bio" daughter Danielle, my "step" daughters Semi and Aleecia, and the love that you no doubt have for your child or children. We owe it to them to be consistently relevant and involved in their lives in the most meaningful way possible.

So how will this book work?

You've experienced the narrative section of the book in this introduction. That's pretty much over.

The rest of this book provides dozens of specific ideas and suggestions as to how you can cultivate and grow your relationship with your child/children even when you don't reside under the same roof.

If you're like me, and most guys, we prefer to see a blueprint vs. a novel when it comes to instructional guides, and so that is how this book is presented - as a straight forward list of things you can start thinking about and doing right away to help build and enhance your relationship with your child/children.

I want you to know that I also recognize that for many Dads it's not a child (singular), but children that we're talking about here.

So, with that in mind, throughout the book when you see a reference to "your child" please know that if you have more than one child you should substitute the word children.

At the same time if you have more than one child, you've probably already figured out by now that they can be very different from one another and are unique in their own individual ways. So always treat them as such. Some ideas and strategies may work better than others depending upon the child.

Part of the fun is figuring and sorting that all out.

Regarding the ideas presented herein you can and should expect this list of suggestions to be honest and direct in its approach. There won't be any pulling of punches or sugar coating of reality.

You don't have time for that.

Finally, as you move through this list of ideas, suggestions, and things to do toward being the best possible "Dad from a Distance", you'll no doubt notice that this list isn't really limited to non-custodial Dads.

I submit to you that many of the ideas listed herein can also work for Step-Dads, Dads who travel a lot, and Dads who reside with, but find themselves at an **emotional** distance from, their child or children.

I think that's because being a great Dad is about more than where you reside and what your legal status is.

It's more about what you choose to do.

This book is about getting on with the business of being a great Dad – starting today!

I hope you'll find what you read here to be helpful.

# Things to Remember

# Things to Think About and Remember

Before we start laying out specific strategies for "things to do" to enhance your role as a Dad and foster a growing relationship with your child, let's first focus on some things that are important to remember.

These "Things to think about and remember" should serve as a backdrop and a foundation for you when you are putting any of the "Things to Do" into practice.

Your successful use of the "Things to Do" strategies depends on 8 very important "Things to Remember".

# Things to Remember #1:

## Remember that your default role with your child is "super-hero"

The built in advantage to being a Dad and a parent in general is that you start off as the greatest influence in your child's life.

They look to you for everything from food to shelter to protection.

You are your child's virtual and actual superhero right from the start.

That role is then yours to keep or lose.

You can keep it by focusing on being the best Dad possible, and consistently doing those things that will get you and keep you there.

# Things to Remember #2:

## It's never too late

Whether you've recently found yourself as a Father from a distance or whether you've been a Father from a distance for a while, it's never too late to make the effort to be actively involved in your child's life.

No doubt, the longer it's been, the more work you'll need to put in, but the big picture is all about forging the most meaningful relationship with your child possible.

Your child is waiting for you to do so.

# Things to Remember #3:

## Mea Culpa helps

If it's taken you a while to get around to doing the Dad thing, consider doing a bit of a Mea Culpa at the beginning of your new effort.

Mea Culpa is a cool Latin phrase that just means to acknowledge your error or guilt.

If you know it's taken too long for you to start actively engaging your child as a Dad, be man enough to say so.

Not only to your child, but to your child's Mother.

Here are some examples of very simple things you can say:

"I should have done this a long time ago. But I want to make things better, and make them right."

"I know I haven't been there for you (your child). And that was wrong. But I'm determined to make it right, and I want to start by saying that I'm sorry."

Once you've done your Mea Culpa, don't be surprised if it's met with some skepticism or even some lingering hostility.

The fact is you may have caused more pain than you know.

However, don't defend, rationalize or retaliate.

This is a time for humility.

You'll need to earn your way through and past the pain, and it will be hard work.

Just remember that you're doing it because you want to forge a meaningful relationship with your child. That realization alone will fuel your efforts and get you through what will at times be a difficult journey.

It will, however, be worth it.

Of that you can be sure.

# Things to remember #4:

## Be consistent

When you launch or re-launch your effort to become more integrally involved in your child's life, one of the most important things you must be is consistent.

Appearing and then disappearing, can actually be more hurtful to your child than you not being there at all. It sends the wrong signal about your reliability and credibility.

Instead, find a way to maintain your effort over the long haul.

You don't have to change the world in a day. In fact, you can't.

But what you can and must do is make your effort to create a great relationship with your child the centerpiece in your life.

Consistency sends the signal to your child that they can count on you, and that's one of the most important aspects of being a great Dad.

Be consistent.

# Things to remember #5:

## Don't give up

I guarantee you that there will be times when you'll feel that your efforts are not getting you anywhere.

Maybe, the child's Mom doesn't seem to be a "believer" in the genuine nature of your efforts or seems to be running interference.

Maybe your child doesn't seem to be impressed by your efforts. Or in general, you just wonder whether it's worth it.

When any of these, or any other frustration occurs, remember why you're doing what you're doing.

When it comes to being a great Dad to your child, nothing should be able to keep you from staying the course.

More than anything else in the world, this effort is worth it, and though you may not see the results or receive the accolades you think you deserve for making the effort, your effort is making a difference in your child's life and in yours.

That's a fact!

So keep at it - Don't give up!

# Things to remember #6

## Don't look for praise or accolades for your efforts

If you're looking to be celebrated and get pats on the back for your efforts, you may be disappointed… at least initially.

The fact is that even the most engaged Dads still take a back seat to Moms.

Instead, keep your eye on the prize – fostering a loving relationship with your child.

It may be a while before you receive any recognition from those folks who'll be looking on. But over time, you'll get the feedback you're looking for from the most important person in the equation – your child.

Even then it may not be verbal.

You'll more readily find it in the look in your child's eye when you are spending time together, and when you see that look, you'll immediately know that it alone will be all the adulation you need.

# Things to remember #7:

## Maintain the correct balance between Dad and Friend.

I'm not one of those people who sees being a Dad and being a friend to your child as being mutually exclusive concepts.

Many of the components to true friendship overlap with concepts that are key to being a great Dad.

Concepts like trust, understanding, fun, open communication, and genuineness are common to both roles.

It's important, however, to accept and embrace that everything you say and do, as a Dad isn't going to engender a happy atmosphere.

Being a good Dad is often more about your child respecting you, and that means there will be times when they don't like you much.

Dads from a distance are sometimes uncomfortable with this because they understand that their time with their child is often limited, and they fear doing or saying anything that will jeopardize a happy but finite time together.

Well, you'll need to get over that.

Part of being a loving parent involves you having to address unacceptable behavior, telling them that yes, they have to do their homework, having them clean up their room and make up their bed, and understanding that you'll sometimes need to say no.

You can expect that your child will on occasion try to test your resolve by attempting to play ends against the middle with you by saying things like "Mom doesn't make me do this", or "Mom says I can do it".

It's important for you to stay in "Dad Mode" and not cave in just to avoid conflict. Giving in just to avoid conflict can and will, over time, create a very difficult environment for the both of you.

Your child may not like you for holding your ground and staying in "Dad Mode" in the short term, but they'll love you and respect you for it in the long term.

# Things to remember #8:

## Focus on just being there

Sometimes, it's not just what you say to or do with your child at any given time that's most important.

What's most important is for them to know that you are there with them, and there for them.

They'll feel this when you create a symphony of behaviors that sends the message on a consistent basis.

Your child wants to know that, above all else, you are there for them.

That's what being a great Dad is really all about, no matter the distance.

# Things to Do

# Things to do

It's important, obviously, that you love your child, but that in and of itself won't be enough – especially from a distance.

And while your loving thoughts are important, it's your actions that really count and demonstrate your love to your child.

Your love for your child will need to be a tangible, touchable series of behaviors, (not just thoughts) on your part that your child can experience with you throughout their lives

Simply put, love is a verb – an action word.

Now that we've laid down a foundation for your successful effort at being a Dad from a Distance with things to think about, let's focus on some things for you to actually do.

There isn't any rhyme or reason to the sequencing of these "Things to Do".

They aren't prioritized or grouped in any special way.

This list also isn't being put forward or promoted as the all inclusive, comprehensive list of everything you could possibly do.

The hope is that you'll find that these ideas spur other ideas in your mind and that this process represents an ongoing spiral upward towards having the most meaningful relationship possible with your child.

Look at this list as a toolbox of ideas on things you can start doing right away to help you maximize your role as a Dad in your child's life.

Remember, love is an action word!

Are you ready? Let's get started!

# Things to Do #1:

## Pay your Child Support

Pay your child support even if you believe the money you are to pay for child support is not being used in a manner that you believe to be appropriate.

The reality of the situation is that you really don't have any say over how the money is being spent or what it's being used for.

More important, however, is the fact that when you don't pay child support, your credibility is damaged on a number of different levels.

First of all, if it's court ordered child support, your failure to pay is unlawful and can lead to a number of legal problems not the least of which is being jailed for being in "Contempt of Court".

There are also financial consequences to not paying child support including your credit rating being damaged and your wages being garnished.

Finally, failure to pay your child support will significantly diminish any atmosphere of cooperation between and your child's Mother.

I can virtually guarantee you that the fact that you aren't paying your child support will be the beginning and end of any conversation with your child's Mom and virtually everyone else who may be in a position to help you.

When you are regularly paying your child support as ordered, it gives you a more firm footing to stand on and creates a less contentious environment to operate in when you're putting forth effort to enhance your relationship with your child.

All that being said, it's not just important to pay child support because of the consequences associated with not doing so.

The most important reason to pay your child support is because it's what responsible Dads do.

# Things to Do #2:

## Never speak ill of your child's Mother, especially in your child's presence

No matter what you think of her, she's still your child's Mother, and anything that you say that is negative or unflattering about her, even in jest, will hurt your child, and reflect negatively on you.

Your child may never tell you this hurts them, but trust me it's a fact. And you can also be sure that your child will remember it for years to come.

It will make spending time with you less desirable and more uncomfortable for your child.

Follow the old adage "if you can't say something nice, don't say anything at all".

Besides, it isn't necessary to denigrate your child's Mom's status to elevate your own.

If your child shares what they believe to be good news about their Mother or what's going on in her life, a simple "Good for her", said without sarcasm or malice, will suffice as an appropriate response.

# Things to Do #3:

## Make it your mission to attend every extracurricular event your child is involved in

Structure your work and budget in such a way that you can be there.

Nothing is quite as wonderful as having your child look up in the stands or out in the audience and see your face.

They want you there, and when you're not, they take notice of that, too.

If you can't be there, make sure your child knows ahead of time so their expectations will be in synch with what actually happens.

Even still, work very hard to make your not being there the exception and not the rule.

Your not being there leaves your child with the impression that they aren't important enough for you to make the effort.

So be there, even if you have to take time off from work without pay.

Be there!

It says to your child "you are important to me!"

# Things to Do #4:

## Join and be an active participant in the PTA, Booster Club, and the other parental involvement organization(s) your child is affiliated with

Being involved at the parental level in organizations that are related to your child's activities not only gives you a way to understand what's going on in their lives, but affords you the opportunity to help shape the experience in a positive way.

It also signals to your child's community that you are an actively engaged parent which can lead to you being in the loop on important issues related to your child's activities.

# Things to Do #5:

## Try to not to let your child's phone call to you go to voice mail, and if it does, return the call with great haste

Children like to talk to you when **they** want to talk to you. Not when it's convenient for you.

If it is the case that you will be unreachable for some reason, make sure your child knows this in advance ("I'll be in a meeting all day on Tuesday" or "I'll be on a plane tomorrow afternoon, so if you call, your call might go to voice mail").

You won't always be available to take their call, but if you can help them know and understand that in advance, they'll get it.

In any case, return the call ASAP. The longer it takes for you to call back, the less interested you'll seem in speaking with your child.

You may also be missing a prime opportunity for your child to express something important and significant to them.

Remember, children like to talk to you when **they** want to talk to you.

Consider, after consulting with your child's Mom, purchasing and paying for a cell phone when your child reaches an appropriate age.

By the way, make sure they, your child and your child's Mom, have a number to reach you in case of emergency.

# Things to Do #6:

## Talk *with* your child at least as much as you talk *to* your child

Actually, more would be better.

Dads are pretty good at giving directions and directives, but not always so great at listening.

Make it your business to ask about your child's day. Ask how they feel about school or friends or activities they are involved in, and when they talk, make sure to listen.

If you make it your goal to listen at least twice as much as you talk, you'll be on the right path to leaving your child with the impression that what they have to say is of value to you.

It will also encourage and make them more comfortable with talking to you about difficult things in the future.

# Things to Do #7:

## Never decline to answer any question your child has for you

Always answer your child's questions, no matter what they are.

You can rest assured that if you don't answer their question, they'll find some else who will, and that may not always be someone who you want to be the source of information or wisdom for your child.

If the question deals with things that you don't believe are age appropriate, you can always say something like "The answer to that question is kind of complicated and will probably make more sense when you're older, but what I *can* tell you is…"

Every time your child asks you a question it provides you both with an opportunity to communicate, and communication is one of the cornerstones of building a great relationship with your child.

# Things to Do #8:

## Take an interest in whatever your child has an interest in

Whether it's sports, video games, science, or dance, take an interest in it.

Dedicate yourself to learning as much as you can about the things your child has an interest in.

Doing so will allow you to share their world with them, and sends the message that what they find important, you find important as well.

Of course to take an interest in what your child is interested in, you have to find out what they are interested in.

How do you find this out?

There's a couple of ways.

1.  Ask your child

2.  Ask your child's Mom

If you don't get an answer, ask again.

Sometimes people assess your genuine interest in something by how persistent and/or consistent you are in pursuing the information.

Keep asking and then when you discover what things interest your child, become a student of what you discover.

Your child will appreciate it, and it will give you another platform from which to grow your relationship.

# Things to Do #9:

## End every phone call and visit with "I love you"

This is a little thing that is a very big thing.

Never let a phone call or a visit end without your child hearing you tell them that you love them.

Don't be discouraged if they don't say it back to you.

You shouldn't be saying it to get a response anyway.

You're saying it so they won't ever be in doubt about the way you feel about them.

# Things to Do #10:

## Attend parent teacher conferences regularly and in concert with your child's Mom

It's important for your child's teachers to know that your child has 2 involved parents, and it's important for your child's Mom to know that as well.

You also will learn what's going on with your child's education and be better positioned to support their educational effort.

# Things to Do #11:

## Do homework with your child even if you have to do it over the phone

There will obviously be times when your child needs help with homework or studying for a test. This is a great time for you to be involved.

You may be thinking, "I wasn't very good at that subject" or "How can I help, when I don't even know what he/she is studying".

Well if you've gotten actively involved in your child's academics, you'll have some clue as to what they are studying and where they may need the most help.

Even if you don't know the subject that well, you can quiz them on what they know.

Just have them fax or email the vocabulary words, the history questions, or whatever they are studying to you and you can quiz them over the phone and help them prepare.

They key here is that this will be easier to do if you are, and continue to be, actively engaged in your child's education.

This is, by the way, something that you can help your child with whether they are in elementary school or college.

Stay tuned in to their education Dad.

It will pay off for them and for you.

# Things to Do #12:

## Volunteer to bring the snacks for your child's team

If your child is on a sports team or is involved in an activity where the parents are tasked with bringing treats or refreshments to practices, games, or performances, step up to the plate and put yourself in the volunteer cycle.

If you don't know what to bring or how much, just ask any other Mom in that group of parents.

They'll be happy to help.

People like to help involved Dad's any way they can.

# Things to Do #13:

## When your child is sick, stay home and care for them

Spending time with your child when he/she is not feeling well is a fundamental part of parenting.

How, you may be thinking, do you set yourself up to be able to do this if you aren't the custodial parent?

Start, by making it known to your child's Mother, that you are willing to take on this role when needed, and have this conversation proactively. Don't wait to talk about it or offer it when your child becomes ill. It will make the logistics of doing it far more difficult for everyone involved.

Let's face it – for a lot of guys, this is unfamiliar territory.

If you are concerned that you won't know what to do, there are 2 sources of information that you can pull from.

First, ask the child's Mom what kinds of medications, if any the child needs to take, and on what schedule. And ask what the best "comfort strategies" (things that tend to make them feel better or more at ease) are for your child.

If your Mom, an aunt, or another maternal figure in your life is accessible to you, she can also be a great source for information as to what to do.

In either case, don't be embarrassed because you're not sure how to care for your sick child.

You don't have time for that.

Your child needs you, and you need to do whatever is necessary to be a viable caregiver when your child isn't feeling well.

And your child will always remember it.

# Things to Do #14:

## Help with school projects

Whether it's a home economics recipe your child is experimenting with, a science project that requires you to collect bugs or anything in between – get involved with their school projects.

Doing school projects with your child makes for a unique and great opportunity to share time, and the project gives you the platform to do so and it comes with it's own agenda.

Friendly word of advice… Remember it's your ***child's*** project so make sure to let ***them*** do the project. You should be acting as an assistant.

Dads are notorious for taking over school projects.

Try not to be that Dad.

# Things to Do #15:

## Celebrate your child's accomplishments with every ounce of energy you have

Whenever your child accomplishes something important to them, no matter how small it may seem, celebrate it with them.

The celebration doesn't have to come in the form of gifts or rewards, although, on occasion that's not a bad idea.

Instead celebrate them by telling them how proud you are of them and expressing confidence in their ability to continue to do great things.

Interestingly, celebrating the "little things" can be even more important than celebrating the bigger milestones.

How will you know when to celebrate them?

That's easy – they'll give you a big hint.

They'll tell you!

Note: Hugs and high fives are definitely acceptable parts of the celebration process!

# Things to Do #16:

## Send postcards when you're out of town

If your job involves traveling, sending postcards is a great way to keep in touch with your child.

It's just another nice reminder to your child that you are thinking of them when you are apart, and has the added benefit of giving your child a broader view of the world.

A postcard in the mail is a special treat when we get one from anyone.

But when a child gets one from Dad – well, that's extra special.

P.S. You don't even have to be out of town to send one!

# Things to Do #17:

## When your child does something worth of your praise, praise them and make it a teachable moment

When your child does something worthy of your praise, not only do you want to make sure you give them praise, but you'll want to reinforce the behavior so that it happens again.

Just the mere act of praise goes a long way toward reinforcement, but you can take steps to make this great teachable Moment.

Here's how:

First, address the behavior as soon as you can - preferably immediately afterward.

Discuss the specifics of what you saw and/or heard with your child.

Discuss with them the positive impact of their behavior – what good outcomes it caused or will cause.

Tell them that you look forward to them doing the same thing in the future when/if the opportunity presents itself.

These simple steps will not only provide praise to your child, but will connect that praise with why the behavior was praiseworthy.

# Things to Do #18:

## When you have to correct your child or offer a critique, make it a teachable moment not just a reprimand

This can be particularly difficult if your child is not used to being "corrected" by you.

The best way to proceed is to focus on the behavior you want to correct, not the attitude that may have come along with it.

Here's how:

First, address the behavior as soon as you can – preferably immediately afterward.

Make sure to have the conversation in private. Don't have it within earshot of anyone else except you and your child.

Discuss the specifics of what you saw and/or heard with your child.

Note: Avoid using words like attitude. They don't speak to specific behavior, but more to how you feel about the behavior.

Discuss with them the negative impact(s) of their behavior – what it caused or could have caused.

Tell them what behavior would have been more appropriate.

Tell them the positive impact(s) of the "replacement" behavior you've suggested – how it could benefit them or make the situation better.

Ask for their commitment to follow through on your suggestion.

If you're consistent with them in how you deal with instances where you need to take corrective action, your child will grow accustomed to it and will learn from it as well.

Don't be surprised if you find them mirroring that same behavior if they feel they need to take corrective action with you.

Don't be offended or be upset, listen and learn from it. Just like you expect them to.

# Things to Do #19:

## Send an e-mail message, a text message, or a greeting card just because

Don't wait for special events or dates to reach out to your child.

Sometimes the most treasured contacts are those that are totally unexpected.

The messages don't have to be long and elaborate. It's probably best that they aren't.

If your child has a cell phone, just sending a text that says something like "I was just thinking of you and wanted to tell you that I love you" will do just fine.

You can do the same thing with e-mail.

As another option, drop by the local card shop and pick up a card in the "Dad to Kid" section, and just write a couple of words inside that express how you feel.

If you can't think of anything to write, something like "I love you" will suffice. Then actually put a stamp on it and mail it to your child.

They'll be excited about it, and will be on the lookout for little contacts from you in the future (so keep it up… Be Consistent, remember?).

They may even send you a couple of cards from time to time.

# Things to Do #20:

## Put your phone on silent when you're with your child

I'm not suggesting that you aren't a busy person, or that you should cut yourself off from all contact with the outside world.

What I am suggesting is that every time your phone rings when you are with your child, your child may see the phone, or rather whoever is calling you, as a competitor for your time.

Your best strategy here is to be proactive.

Tell the people close to you that you are with your child during whatever time period is the case, and that if they call you they can/should expect their call to go to voice mail. Let them know you'll call them back as soon as possible, but it may be a while.

If you are expecting a call that is very important, let your child know this ahead of time, and assure them that you will keep it short because your time together is important.

You can return phone calls when there is a break in the action – when your child goes to sleep, or is caught up in a TV show.

The key here is to make sure that your phone doesn't put a damper on the special time you get to spend with your child.

# Things to Do #21:

## Make sure everyone close to you understands that your child is your priority

It's very important, if not critical, that everyone close to you understand that your child is a major priority in your life.

Anyone who has a problem with that probably shouldn't be close to you.

Your child should never feel as though they are in competition for your love and affection.

And you should never be in a position to have to justify that love and affection to anyone close to you.

If you have even the slightest feeling that having your child as a priority in your life is or will be a problem for anyone in your social circle, consider moving that person outside your social circle.

# Things to Do #22:

## Never miss a birthday, Christmas, or Valentine's Day

While this seems like a no-brainer, it's easy to get caught up in our busy lives and let important dates slip up on us.

Make a point of mentally moving these dates up by 2 weeks.

That will give you time to buy something and/or send a card so that it arrives in time or early.

A gift or a card that arrives even 1 day late, no matter what people say, loses some of its luster.

It can make the receiver (i.e. your child) feel as though they were an afterthought.

Make sure your child knows that you have forethought enough to recognize their very special days by taking care of your gift buying and card sending early.

# Things to Do #23:

## Make Father's day a day you recognize and celebrate with your child

The day wouldn't mean anything to you if not for your child.

Consider giving them a gift for the day to celebrate your very special bond.

If this day doesn't fall on your weekend or during your summer visitation, make every attempt to reschedule or swap weekends well in advance or at the very least spend Father's day Sunday together.

# Things to Do #24:

## Take lots of pictures and video

It's not unusual for Fathers, especially those recently separated from their children, not to have much of a photo archive of your child.

You can do something about that.

Make a point of taking pictures at events and times, both big and small, to capture your child's image.

If you don't have a digital camera, buy one, even if it's a cheap model, and start taking pictures.

You'll never believe how fast the time goes by and how quickly they grow up, so create your own picture history.

Make sure to share those pictures with them and grandparents and everyone else who has a stake in the growth and development of your child.

There's nothing quite as fun as looking back on those pictures later in life.

You'll not only recall the when and where of the photos, but you'll also flash back to how great the feeling was you had at the time… and so will your child.

# Things to Do #25:

## Build in as much grandma and grandpa time as you can

Your parents need to be a vital part of your child's life, so make sure to build in time for visits to see them.

Children cherish the special bond with their grandparents.

Make it your business to make sure they get that quality time.

A note of caution here; don't make your child's grandparents their "all the time" babysitters.

That's not their job.

The point is to make sure that you do everything you can to help foster a loving relationship between your child and your parents.

# Things to Do #26:

## Read to your child, if only over the phone

As silly as it sounds, reading to your child over the phone is a fantastic way to spend quality time with your child.

In fact, go to the bookstore and let your child pick the book when you are together, and then read a chapter or two whenever you speak to them over the phone.

Your child will look forward to these shared moments and you will too.

# Things to Do #27:

## A day at the park or at a museum can make for a great day too

Plan activities that create memories.

Most towns and cities have free events each week and you can learn about them from your local newspaper (hardcopy or online).

Look for opportunities to attend festivals, concerts, museums, etc.

Activities at these types of venues can not only create great memories, but can be very economical as well.

# Things to Do #28:

## When you're wrong, say so

You can bet, that even with your best efforts that you'll make a mistake.

If you find that you're wrong about something, make sure to acknowledge it to your child.

Too often, rather than just admitting that we're wrong about something, we spend a great deal of effort on justifying what we did or rationalizing it (as if that changes the facts).

When you demonstrate that you are a big enough person to acknowledge that you're wrong, you are, at the same time, teaching your child to follow your example.

# Things to Do #29:

## When you cause hurt, apologize

For many people, "I apologize", or "I'm sorry" are difficult if not impossible to give voice too.

But life is not perfect and neither are you.

There will come a time, if it hasn't come already, that you will do or say something, no matter how unintentional that will hurt your child's feelings.

The moment you realize that's the case, apologize.

Don't wait. Don't hesitate.

Apologizing is one of the purest ways of showing that you care about someone and their feelings.

It also shows strength of character.

A Dad who apologizes teaches his child that it's appropriate to apologize when the occasion calls for it.

# Things to Do #30:

## When your child does even the smallest kindness for you, say "Thank you"

Children have some of the most unique ways of saying they love you.

They are likely to do everything from pull a flower (or weed) from the lawn and giving it to you, to drawing you a picture.

Whatever it is that your child says to you, or does for you to express their love is a big deal and should be treated as such.

Put that flower (or weed) in a keepsake book, put the picture they drew you or the note they wrote you on the refrigerator.

Make sure that your child understands clearly how much you appreciate any little kindness or expression of love they show you.

It will not only please them, but it will encourage more of the same.

# Things to Do #31:

## If your child misses your birthday, or Father's day, or any other special day for you, keep your hurt to yourself

Rest assured they already feel bad enough. Forgive them and move on.

There could be a number of reasons why they missed the day. The important thing is that you not make a big deal out of it.

Remember, a forgiving Dad raises forgiving children.

# Things to Do #32:

## Make encouragement the centerpiece of every conversation about their hopes, and dreams, and their failures and disappointments

This may seem like an obvious thing, but it's so important that it's listed here, as it's own suggestion.

There are few things as powerful as a Dad telling their child that they believe in them – Especially when they stumble and fall, both literally and figuratively.

It's as simple as uttering little phrases like:

"You'll get 'em next time"

"Don't give up"

"I believe in you"

"I'm proud of you, no matter what"

When your child has run into an obstacle in their life, it means the world to them to know that they have you in their corner; rooting them on through and past whatever setback they've experienced.

Be an encourager at every opportunity.

# Things to Do #33:

## When you feel angry, delay is your most effective ally

Obviously, everything your child does will not make you happy.

In fact some of it will make you downright angry.

When you find yourself feeling this way, your best strategy is to give yourself some time to cool down.

It's like the direction you may have been given when you were a child – "count to ten".

It will give you a clearer head and help you address the situation with less angry words and actions.

Remember, your time with your child may be limited, meaning you may not have time to "fix it" if you say or do the wrong thing in anger.

So give it some time, and then address the situation with a cooler head.

Not only will this help you communicate on a much better level with your child, you will at the same time be teaching them, through your example, how to handle things when **they** are angry.

# Things to Do #34:

## Keep a picture of your child close and look at it often

Whether you keep it in your wallet or on your cell phone, it will remind you of what's really important in life.

As an additional idea, ask your child to put their picture on your phone or make their picture the wallpaper on the home screen of your cell phone (there's a good chance that they know how to do this better than you).

If you happen to be having a particularly difficult day, looking at your child's picture will lift your spirits.

Remembering that you're a Dad can have that affect on you.

# Things to Do #35:

## Have a portrait photo taken of just you and your child

Arrange to have a professional portrait taken of just you and your child.

We're not talking here of having someone just take a picture of the two of you on your cell phone camera or something that just happens on the spur of the moment.

Those are great, too, but we're talking about something a little different here.

We're talking about having a very nice portrait of you and your child taken professionally.

It's not a hugely expensive endeavor, and you can even get it done in many shopping malls.

Make sure to really take some time and make the effort to make it a special event by dressing up a bit.

Make a trip to the barber for you, and sponsor and/or take your child to the barber or hairdresser.

Even plan a nice lunch or dinner out afterwards.

The outcome will be a treasured experience and a keepsake you'll have for the rest of your lives.

It'll be more than just simply a picture; it'll be your own Family Portrait.

# Things to Do #36:

## Put a picture of your child in a prominent place in your home

You want your child to know that they are front and center in your world even when they aren't physically there with you.

Putting up a picture in a prominent place in your home sends your child the signal that not only are you acknowledging their presence, but that you are doing so proudly and boldly for all the world to see.

It will help remind your child how important they are in your life and that means a lot to them.

# Things to Do #37:

## Buy your child enough clothes and toiletries so that when they come to visit, they won't have to "pack" first

This can make life much easier for your child and can make the visit seem less like a "trip" and more like a visit.

This also allows for more spontaneity in your child's visits if the opportunity arises.

When your child has their "own stuff" permanently at your place it helps makes your place feel not just like your home.

It will make them feel as though it's their home, too.

# Things to Do #38:

## Spend time alone with your child

While it is often fun to share your time with your child with others, it is very important that you also spend time with just them – Just the two of you alone.

The time that you have with them is at a premium and it is also limited time.

This doesn't make you selfish. It makes it clear that sometimes, it really should be about your time together.

# Things to Do #39:

## Don't crowd your child or try to compete with the other parent

Focus on Quality not Quantity.

Competition would be less about your child and more about your issues with the other parent.

Don't burden your child with this.

They've been burdened enough by the separation.

# Things to Do #40:

## Use SKYPE or other on-line video tools to have "face-time" with your child

The wonderful thing about technology is that there are now so many on-line tools that you can use to keep in touch, and many of them are free to use.

One of those tools is called SKYPE.

SKYPE has become popular because of its use on TV shows and even in news reporting.

It allows you to actually see the person that you're talking to on-line, and they can see you too.

It's a wonderful tool because it lets you experience not just a voice or text, but facial expressions as well.

Best of all, it's free!

You will need a high-speed internet connection, and a video cam. If you don't have a video cam built in to your computer, your local office supply or box store (Best Buy, Wal-Mart, Target, etc) sell them and they don't cost a lot.

Get "SKYPE" and take advantage of another great way to stay connected.

# Things to Do #41:

## Use online instant messaging tools to keep in touch

There are a number of free services available that allow you to send and receive instant messages to and from you child.

Depending on your child's age, there's a good possibility that they already have an instant messaging account. If that's the case, find out which one they are using and set up an account on that same service and get connected.

If they don't have an instant messaging account, set up one together.

There are a number of companies that make free instant messaging available: AOL Instant Messaging, Yahoo Messaging, and MSN Messenger, just to name a few.

Instant messaging is just another cool and cost effective way to stay in touch and communicate with your child from a distance.

# Things to Do #42:

## Make sure your child knows that you have high expectations for them

Most people tend to live up to (or down to) our expectations of them.

The same holds true for your child, and while making you angry may not be a big deal for them, disappointing you is.

Consider this as an approach.

Rather than telling them you expect all A's in school, or that they should be the fastest member of the track team, consider setting your expectations for them on a more personal level.

Tell them that you always expect them to do their best.

It's not about always having them be **the** best, just to have them to always do **their** best that's important.

Being the best may not always be possible, but doing their best is.

So in times of disappointment, when they don't feel great about an outcome in their life, the question from Dad can always simply be "Did you do your best?"

If the answer is yes, then they've done what you've expected of them, and that's a pretty good thing.

By the way, doing your best is also a great goal for you as a Dad.

Just a thought…

# Things to Do #43:

## Create a savings account for them and contribute to it regularly

We're talking about something apart from child support here.

Not only will creating some type of savings account benefit your child later in life, you'll feel better as you see it grow.

It's as easy as setting up a custodial account at your local bank.

If you don't have the discipline to remember to contribute to the account on your own, make it an automatic process through your bank.

In fact, you could even set up a joint account at a local brokerage house and grow an account for your child there via investments.

It can then be an excellent teaching tool for children later in life as to how to manage and care for their own money.

The point here is not to have something to brag about to the world and hold up as evidence that you're a great Dad.

Rather, the point is to do something great for your child that no one has to know about but you.

Besides, great Dads don't have to brag about being great Dads.

Their actions and behavior speak for them.

# Things to Do #44:

## Celebrate your child "behind their back"

Your child doesn't always have to see or hear you celebrate them.

Talk about your child's accomplishments to friends and family.

If you're on Facebook, share their big moments and your shared big moments in the status of your home page.

The positive reinforcement you'll get from friends and family will put wind in your sails and encourage you to keep doing great Dad stuff.

As an added benefit, your child will be thrilled to hear from others how much you celebrate them and their accomplishments, and how proud you are of them.

# Things to Do #45:

## If there is ever something you feel you should have said…

No matter what it is, make it your business and priority to get it said…. Right away.

Enough said.

# Things to Do #46:

## Be civil towards your child's Mom whenever you're all present

Maintaining an air of civility is important to do even if your child isn't present. And you should do so no matter how you feel about your child's Mom or her behavior.

It's about making sure your child always sees you taking the "High Road".

You'll be modeling the proper behavior and at the same time teaching your child how to behave even when they don't get along with someone well.

Not only will your child remember and appreciate it, it may even help inoculate them from any negative messaging that may be coming their way about you.

# Things to Do #47:

## Take your child out Trick or Treating or Easter Egg Hunting, or to their friend's birthday parties, etc.

Especially for younger children, few things are as fun as these activities.

Take advantage of these as opportunities to spend some great quality time with your child in settings that are custom fit just for them.

To make it an even richer experience, plan the whole experience with your child – from selecting Halloween costumes to wear, coloring eggs, to choosing birthday gifts for their friends.

It may not seem like a big deal, but these are just a few more examples of how you can signal to your child that they are important.

Remember, nothing sends the "importance" signal quite like spending time together.

# Things to Do #48:

## Avoid making your child your messenger to their Mom

It's possible that communication between you and child's Mom might be strained at times or, at the very least, somewhat uncomfortable.

This can make it very tempting to use your child as a messenger to their Mom.

Avoid doing this for a couple of reasons.

First, it puts your child in the middle of the issues between you and their Mom. That's not a place they belong.

Secondly, even if they don't tell you, it's an uncomfortable role they'd rather not play.

This is your child we're talking about here, not a carrier pigeon.

Additionally, mutual friends, your family, your child's Mother's friends and relatives, and any other potential messengers are also usually unwilling participants in the messenger game; so spare them too.

Handle your own communications with your child's Mom.

If face-to-face communications or phone calls aren't working well, agree to communicate (except in cases of emergency) via e-mail, text, or by some other means.

Just make sure whatever strategy you come up with doesn't involve your child.

Their job is to be your child… and that's it.

# Things to Do #49:

## Consider having a bedroom, fully furnished, for your child at your home

Even though your child's stay with you may be temporary, your home can feel like a place that's always there for them.

Having a single drawer in a dresser or the floor in a sparsely furnished spare room for their stuff doesn't do that.

Your child having their own bed, and dresser, and closet does do that.

Yes it will cost money, and yes it will only be used sparingly. But it sends the signal to your child that your dwelling is not just a place they spend a couple of nights from time to time.

Instead, it says, "This is your home, too".

Don't think of it as an added expense. Rather, think of it as a meaningful investment in your relationship with your child.

# Things to Do #50:

## Spend time laughing with your child

Kids like "silly" sometimes (even older kids). It's important for your child to know that fun is a part of your make-up.

Make sure that while you take your role as Dad seriously, you don't take yourself too seriously.

# Things to Do #51:

## Never be late picking your child up for your visitation time

Do whatever it takes to be on time to pick your child up for your visitation.

Rest assured, your child will be watching the clock and every moment you're late can be interpreted as a lack of interest on your part.

Plus, being on time shows consideration for your child's Mom as well, and while that might not mean much to you, I guarantee your child will be taking notice.

# Things to Do #52:

## Write your child a letter on occasion and mail it to them the old fashioned way

Writing a simple letter to your child gives you another way to express yourself to them, and it will give your child something from you to treasure and keep.

Tell them about your day.

Tell them about what you've got planned next time you're together.

Tell them again how much they mean to you.

If you think you're not much of a writer, and wouldn't be able to do this, just give it a try.

You'll find more words pouring from your pen and your heart than you even knew were there.

Your child's receiving a letter from you will make their day, and it will make your day too.

# Things to Do #53:

## Ride the train

This may seem to be completely off the wall and spontaneous suggestion, but it can also be a lot of fun for you and your child.

In some malls and at some amusement parks there are train rides available to take with smaller (and larger) children.

Consider even taking a ride on the public rail system in your city or even on Amtrak if those options are available to you. They can make for an inexpensive way to spend time and see your hometown from a different point of view.

While an older child may not be as interested, younger children tend to be fascinated by trains and the thought of riding on one.

So if you get the opportunity, take your child on a train ride.

They'll really enjoy it, and you will too.

All aboard!

# Things to Do #54:

## Visit the local carnival

On occasion a traveling carnival may set up shop in your hometown.

You'll recognize it as the one that you typically hope your child doesn't notice as you drive by.

Rather than using diversionary tactics to distract them from looking over and seeing the carnival, consider spontaneously stopping by to visit.

Between the Ferris wheel, the cotton candy, and the prize booths, you'll find that you and your child will have a great time together.

You may even win them a prize as part of the bargain, but even if you don't, the memory will stand as a memento of another great time you've shared together.

# Things to Do #55:

## Take them to get pictures with Santa, and the Easter Bunny

There's no rule that says only Moms can take their child to get those great pictures with Santa or the Easter Bunny.

And it really doesn't matter how old they are.

Getting the picture taken could be a great experience that could range from anything to great excitement to great silliness.

Want to make it even more interesting?

Consider you being in the picture too!

# Things to Do #56:

## Have movie nights at home, complete with popcorn and lights out

Let your child pick a movie to watch, and then make an event of it at your home, complete with popcorn, snacks and lights out.

It doesn't matter whether you want to see the movie they picked or not.

The point is you'll be creating an atmosphere *with* them and not *for* them that will allow you to spend some low maintenance, low cost, high quality time together.

Like many of the suggestions in this book, pre-planning activities with your child really adds value to the time you spend together.

In fact, the further out you plan for movie night, the greater the anticipation will be which will only add to creating the atmosphere for a great time together.

# Things to Do #57:

## Take walks

It's amazing what you find to talk about when you're out for a stroll.

It can be a walk around your neighborhood or at a park in the community. It really doesn't matter where.

Make it at least 30 minutes.

Not only will you have spent some real quality time with your child – you will have contributed to your child's health and fitness and your own.

# Things to Do #58:

## Take some time off from work if you have an extended visitation period

It's not uncommon for court ordered visitation to have some period of the year when you'll have a month to six weeks of uninterrupted visitation.

This is often scheduled in the summer.

Many Dads are equal parts happy about and anxious about this period of time, and what to do with it.

Avoid letting this special time turn into just a boring routine of your child waiting for you to come home from work every day.

Instead, consider taking some vacation time and spending every moment you can enjoying this special time with your child.

What better way to spend your vacation than with your child!

You don't have to go somewhere expensive or extravagant. You don't even have to leave town.

Take some of the "what to do" anxiety out of the equation by putting together a plan in advance.

Better yet, let your child help you plan your time together. In fact, if they are old enough to do so, let your child take the lead in the planning process.

You may be surprised how creative the plan can become with you working together on it.

Not only will this give them ownership in the plan, it will add to the anticipation of your time together which can really boost how much fun you'll have.

The point is that this may be one of the rare opportunities you have each year to spend an extended amount of time with your child.

Take full advantage of it.

# Things to Do #59:

## Be part of teaching them how to drive

One of the most pivotal times in a young person's life is when they learn how to drive.

The experience is full of excitement and nervous energy and, as such, a great time for a Dad's presence.

Being part of this important time is a great way to spend quality time and strengthen your bond with your child.

You can be involved in everything from taking them to get their learner's permit to coaching them on their driving skills in an empty parking lot.

Think of how great it would be for you to be standing by waiting for them after they've completed their road test – Either to congratulate them when they pass and get their license or to offer words of encouragement if they don't.

While your involvement may not include every aspect of the process, any involvement you have will be significant and will create a series of memories that will always be with both of you.

# Things to Do #60:
## Learn something new with your child

It can be tennis, bowling, golf, another language, fishing… it doesn't really matter what it is.

Learning something from scratch for the both of you will give you a truly unique experience that will be worth a lifetime of memories.

Add even more value to the experience by letting your child participate in the decision as to what you'll be learning together.

You'll find out that you won't just be learning about the new thing. You'll be learning about each other at the same time.

# Things to Do #61:

## Take your child to their doctor and dentist appointments when you can

You should know the health care professionals who take care of your child and they should know who you are, too.

Also, you should always be clearly informed as to the status of your child's health and be aware of everything you need to be doing to help them stay healthy.

Taking your child to their Dentist and Doctor appointments will allow you to do this in an informed way.

It also provides yet another signal to your child that they matter and are important to you.

# Things to Do #62:

## Visit college campuses together

A great way to spend time with your child that will also positively affect their vision for the future is to take them to visit a college campus.

Chances are, there is a college campus near you, and if not, a campus visit can be a great opportunity for a road trip.

This presents you with yet another opportunity to let your child participate in the decision making process by getting their input on which college they might like to visit.

Ultimately, however, it doesn't really matter which school you choose.

Just pick one and go!

Consider calling ahead to the admissions office and ask to speak to a recruiter for the school. They may even be able to arrange a tour of the campus.

A trip to a college campus gives your child a glimpse into what the future may hold for them and that vision will include you.

# Things to Do #63:

## Do a joint project around your home

There's nothing quite like a project around the house to create special and often times humorous memories.

Consider a project like painting their room or building something together, and have your child be part of the project from planning to completion.

Even if it is a project that takes place over a number of weekends, it's ok.

The completed project will be something that you created and accomplished together and every time your child sees it, they'll be reminded that it was something you did together.

# Things to Do #64:

## Attend a place of worship together

It can be a very rich experience to attend worship services with your child.

Not only is it "together time", it is also an opportunity to reinforce a strong moral set of values for your child and for you, too.

It is a wonderful thing for your child to hear the messages that you've conveyed to them come from another source and not only does it serve to reinforce your messages to your child, it reinforces your credibility in their eyes as well.

Take the day's message and use it in conversation with your child and in so doing, you can help give the message real world relevance in your child's life, and your own.

Even if you and your child don't attend worship services together, there are a number of events that call for a Dad's attendance, including Baptisms, Confirmations, Holiday plays, and more.

While the examples I've cited reflect milestones common to Christianity, every Faith has celebrated rites of passage and milestones.

No matter your faith, your presence is what is key here.

As an added bonus, most places of worship also have numerous activities and organizations that you and your child can join and participate in together.

# Things to Do #65:

## Attend every Graduation Ceremony

Nowadays, it seems that there are lots of opportunities to attend graduation ceremonies.

It's not uncommon for there to be such ceremonies for Kindergarten, Middle School, and High School – not to mention College and Graduate School.

You should make it your business to be at each and every one of these educational milestones in your child's life.

It gives them great joy to see you there and it disappoints and hurts them if you're not – even if they never tell you so.

It also demonstrates and signals to your child that you value education.

Not sure when the ceremonies take place?

Remember, if you're consistently involved with your child's schools and their teachers, you'll be sure to be in the loop.

Remember to take lots of pictures!

# Things to Do #66:

## Be there on Prom Night

Few events are as significant in your child's life as Prom Night.

Make arrangements with your child's Mom for you to be there before your son or daughter begins their evening.

It's a great time for picture taking, celebration, and offering some "Fatherly" advice.

You don't get a lot of opportunities to be part of something like Prom Night, so make it your business to do everything in your power to be present and accounted for on this very special evening in your child's life.

# Things to Do #67:

## Go fly a kite

Nothing is quite like the fun you can have with your child as going out to the park and flying kites together.

It seems sometimes to be a bit of a lost art, but you can still likely find kites in stores in your community, and, if you're really feeling adventurous, go on line and get instructions for building a kite from scratch.

Whichever kite acquisition plan you choose, be sure to involve your child in the process.

If you've never flown a kite before, it can be even more fun for you to learn to fly one together.

Kite flying is inexpensive, high-energy fun that you can share.

So next time when someone tells you to "Go fly a kite", thank them for the suggestion.

# Things to Do #68:

## Go on a picnic together

Picnics provide a fun way to spend quality time that's custom made for time together with your child.

Let your child help you plan what the meal will be for your picnic, and remember to take a blanket, cups, plates, and plenty of good food to eat. You might even want to bring along some music to listen to.

To make the time together even more fun and engaging, consider taking a board game or a deck of cards along to play together.

Just in case, take a small trash bag with you and set a proper example on how to keep the park beautiful for others to enjoy.

# Things to Do #69:

## Help your child shop for their Mom for significant gift giving occasions

Your child, especially when they are younger, won't have the means or resources to shop for their Mom on special days like birthdays, Mother's Day, Christmas, or even Valentine's Day.

These are however very important days not only for your child's Mom but for your child as well.

It's important to children to show their love to their Moms on days such as these, and helping them in this effort is a significant demonstration of not only how great a Dad you are, but how big a Man you are.

We're not talking diamonds and gold here. It's obvious that whatever you help your child buy should be within reason. The fact is that your child is more interested in getting a gift for their Mom than with how much it costs. Even if your financial situation limits you to taking your child to a greeting card shop to buy their Mom a card, do it.

Helping your child in this very important way will say to your child that you love them in a way that few other gestures can.

# Dad from a Distance "Meals"

# Dad from a Distance Meals

## Being a great Dad from a Distance also includes being a Dad in the kitchen every once in a while

This section of the book actually comes as the result of an excellent observation made by my very smart wife, Melodie.

She noted that a lot of the Dads we're discussing in this book (and remember, I was and am still am one of them) rarely prepare meals at home with their kids.

As a result, breakfast, lunch, and dinner very often (if not always) take place in a restaurant somewhere or are the result of "take-out" or "drive thru". And while the kids may get a kick out of eating out all the time with Dad (that and the fact that these are quick and easy options) it can also become very expensive over time.

Her very valid point was that spending quality time with your child can and should also, on occasion, include preparing meals at home that are fun, easy and economical.

Given that a lot of guys who live alone may not even have any direct proof that their stoves even work (smile), we thought it might be helpful to include in this book a few meals that you can enjoy preparing with your child or that can be prepared ahead of time for easy heat and eat enjoyment at home.

This section of the book is my wife's gracious, well qualified, and very much appreciated contribution to this effort – mainly because I'm way out of my league on this topic (Thanks Sweetheart!).

Before you get started there are a few basic kitchen tools (pots/pans and utensils) and basic seasoning that you should keep on hand whether you are cooking in preparation of your child's visit or just for yourself.

Buy yourself a basic set of pots and pans. These can be purchased separately or as a boxed set that typically includes both a 1 and 2 quart sized pan, 1 or 2 frying pans/skillets and 1 large stock/ soup pot with lids.

Also purchase the kitchen utensil set that will include spatula, large cooking fork, spoons, ladles etc. A strainer or colander along with a cutting board and set of mixing bowls are also basics that you want to include in your kitchen.

You will also need the following basic spices: salt, pepper, onion powder, garlic powder, oregano, seasoning salt, old bay seasoning, sugar, minced garlic, chicken bouillon/stock and butter. Having vegetable oil and a can of spray oil (Pam or store brand) is also advised. Once you have these basics you can expand your seasoning collection as your culinary skills advance.

On the following pages, you'll find a few basic meals and recipes that you can enjoy with your child. At the end of each recipe, we've included a shopping list to copy/write down to take with you to the grocery store.

In some cases it may be easier and or more economical to purchase the items already prepared and just add the main course or sides. Options will be provided for your consideration along with recipes and cooking instructions. Enjoy!

Hint: Read through the entire menu and preparation instructions. Write down all ingredients required to complete the meal. Check your cabinets and refrigerator to see what you already have and what you need to purchase prior to getting in the car. The shopping experience can also be an adventure that can be shared with your child. You will learn some of their culinary likes and dislikes in preparation for the next meal.

# Dad from a Distance Meal #1:

Fish Sticks or Fish Nuggets/Filets

Tater tots, French Fries, Baked Potato

Salad with Salad Dressing or Green Beans

Iced tea, Crystal Light, Milk or water

Dessert: Jell-O/Jell-O Pudding

## Preparation Instructions:

**Fish Sticks** – Purchase from the frozen food section and follow the directions on the package.

**Fish Nuggets/Filets** – Purchase fresh fish of your choice from the seafood section of your local grocery store.

Prep: Season with a little salt, pepper and old bay seasoning. Spray bottom of frying pan with Pam/spray oil, or use 2 tablespoons of vegetable oil heated over a medium high heat. Place fish in pan for approximately 3–5 minutes on each side. Depending on the thickness of the fish, it could take a little longer (your local butcher can assist with the cooking time as well as other preparation options).

Option: You may purchase a fish batter coating/seasoning and follow box instructions.

**Tater tots/French fries** – Purchase from the frozen food section and follow the directions on the package. You can add seasoning salt for variety.

**Or Baked Potato** – Purchase baking potatoes from the produce/ vegetable section of the grocery store. Potatoes are sold either separately or in 5 or 10 pound bags.

Pre-heat the oven to 425 degrees. Wash the potatoes under running water and make sure the dirt has been removed. Cover a cookie sheet with aluminum foil (if you don't have a cookie sheet, place potatoes on foil directly on the rack in the oven once prepared). Pierce the potato with a fork. Spray or coat the potatoes with oil and place in the oven for 30 to 45 minutes. Test for doneness by inserting a toothpick, or fork into the potato (the potato should be soft throughout).

**Salad** – Can be purchased in a bag ready to eat in the produce section, or purchase, lettuce, tomato, shredded carrots etc. Chop lettuce, tomato place into a bowl, and toss in shredded carrots. Top with salad dressing.

**Green Beans** – Purchase canned green beans from the vegetable aisle or frozen green beans from the freezer section.

Frozen green beans can be purchased with seasoning or butter already in the package and can just be popped in the microwave per the instructions on the package.

Canned green beans should be drained of their liquid and heated on the stove in a quart pan with about ½ cup of water, 1 teaspoon of minced garlic, a little salt and pepper and butter. Chicken bullion or stock can be substituted for the water and garlic.

**Dessert** - Jell-O or Jell-O Pudding can be purchased in single serving cups in the dairy section or can be prepared from a box typically located on the baking aisle. If preparing from a box follow the instructions found on the box.

# Dad from a Distance Meal #1:

## Grocery Shopping List

○ Fish Sticks *or* Fish Filet/Nuggets

○ Tater Tots *or* French Fries *or* Baking Potatoes

○ Prepared Salad in a Bag

    *or* for Homemade Salad

       ○ Lettuce

       ○ Tomato

       ○ Shredded Carrots

       ○ Cucumbers

○ Salad Dressing of your choice

○ Green Beans – Canned *or* Frozen

○ Jell-O/Jell-O Pudding ready made, *or* Jell-O/Jell-O Pudding Mix

○ Milk (if making Jell-O Pudding from Mix)

# Dad from a Distance Meal #2:

Spaghetti & Meat Sauce

Corn

Salad

Rolls

Iced tea, Crystal Light, Milk or water

Ice cream cup

## Preparation Instructions:

**Spaghetti** – Purchase spaghetti from the pasta aisle. Follow instructions on the box to prepare. Once rinsed and drained, set-aside in a bowl, with ½ cup water with a little melted butter. This will keep the noodles from sticking together.

**Meat Sauce** – 1 pound of ground beef or ground turkey (meat section). Season meat with a little salt, pepper, garlic and onion powder. In large frying pan brown meat over medium to medium-high heat, stirring with large long handle fork (break up larger pieces with fork while cooking). Drain or spoon off fat/grease and discard. Add one large jar, 28–32 oz of prepared spaghetti sauce (Ragu, Classico, Paul Newman). Tomato Basil, or Tomato with Garlic and Onion style sauce is recommended. Add about ¼ teaspoon of salt, pepper, onion and garlic powder to the sauce and 1 teaspoon oregano. Stir together and let simmer on low heat for 30 minutes.

**Corn** – Purchase canned corn from the canned vegetable aisle or frozen corn from the freezer section. Drain canned corn and add ½ cup of water, a little salt and pepper and 1 tablespoon of butter/margarine heat over medium heat in a small saucepan. Frozen corn can be purchased with or without seasoning. Follow microwave or stovetop instructions provided on the package. If seasoning is required, add a little butter, salt, and pepper.

**Rolls** – Purchase heat and serve rolls located on the bread aisle and follow the package cooking directions. Or use Hawaiian Sweet Rolls, which require no heating.

**Dessert** – Purchase either individual ice cream cups, which are typically sold in vanilla or chocolate flavors only, or purchase a quart or half gallon of the family favorite.

# Dad from a Distance Meal #2:

## Grocery Shopping List

- ○ Spaghetti Noodles

- ○ 1lb of meat (Ground Beef *or* Ground Turkey)

- ○ 1 Jar (26–32 oz) prepared Tomato Basil Spaghetti Sauce

- ○ Canned Corn *or* Frozen Corn

- ○ Prepared Salad in a Bag,

  *or* for Homemade Salad

  - ○ Lettuce

  - ○ Tomato

  - ○ Shredded Carrots

  - ○ Cucumbers

- ○ Salad Dressing of your choice

- ○ Heat and Serve Rolls *or* Hawaiian Sweet Rolls

- ○ Ice Cream Cups *or* ½ Gallon of Ice Cream

# Dad from a Distance Meal #3:

Grilled Ham and Cheese Sandwich

Soup (cup or bowl)

Carrot Sticks/Pickle or Pickle Slices

Iced tea, Crystal Light, Milk or water

Popsicle

## Preparation Instructions:

**Grilled Ham and Cheese** – 2 slices of white or wheat bread per sandwich, 1 slice of American cheese, and one slice of ham sandwich meat.  Spread a thin coating of softened butter on both sides of the bread, add cheese and ham and close with the other slice of bread. Place one or more sandwiches in the frying pan (medium to medium high heat), for approximately 3 minutes on each side. With a spatula lift corner to check for toasting of bread. If the bread is browning too fast turn the heat down to ensure the cheese melts and the ham heats.

Option: Ham and Cheese sandwich with a little mayo, mustard, lettuce and tomato.

**Soup** – Purchase favorite soup from the canned soup aisle and follow heating instructions provided.

**On the Side** – Add carrot sticks or baby carrots located in the produce section or a whole pickle or a few dill pickle slices, which can be found on the condiments aisle.

**Dessert** – Pick up some frozen popsicles in the freezer section.

# Dad from a Distance Meal #3:

## Grocery Shopping List

○ Sandwich Bread (White or Wheat)

○ American Cheese Slices

○ Thin sliced Deli Ham (from the Deli or Sandwich Meat Section)

○ Soup of choice

○ Baby Carrots **or** Carrot Sticks

○ Jar of Dill Pickles (Whole or Sliced)

○ Frozen Popsicles

# Dad from a Distance Meal #4:

Pork Chops

Steamed Cabbage *or* Broccoli

Macaroni and Cheese

Iced tea, Crystal Light, Milk or water

Fruit and/or Flavored Yogurt

## Preparation Instructions:

**Pork Chops** – From the meat section, purchase bone-in pork chops or pork chop filets. Trim fat and season with a little salt, pepper, garlic and onion powder. Heat frying pan with 2 tablespoons of vegetable oil (or coat pan with cooking spray), to medium high heat level. Add pork chops and brown on both sides for 5–7 minutes.

Options: Pick up a package of pork gravy mix (dry mix) or a jar of pork gravy and add to chops after you have browned on both sides and let simmer for 10 minutes. To spice things up add sliced onion and sliced green/red bell peppers while browning the pork chops.

**Steamed Cabbage** – Purchase one small head of cabbage from the produce section as well as one onion and a package of bacon.  Quarter the cabbage and remove the stem/core. Slice cabbage into ½" width strips and rinse and drain excess water. Slice onion and set aside. Take 4 or 5 strips of bacon (whole or slices into smaller pieces) and fry in the soup/stock pot over a medium high heat. This will provide you with bacon fat/drippings for flavor. Once the bacon is crisp, add ½ the cabbage and ½ the onion. Season with salt, pepper, garlic and onion powder. Repeat with the other ½ of cabbage and onion and seasonings. Add ½ teaspoon of sugar and ½ cup of water. Reduce heat to medium, cover, and let simmer for 15 minutes (adding more water if needed), stir, cover, and continue to simmer for approximately 15 minutes or until desired doneness.

Veggie Option: Steamed broccoli or broccoli and cheese which can be picked up in the frozen food section. Just follow heating directions on package.

**Macaroni and Cheese** – This too can be purchased in the frozen food section with quick microwave or oven heating directions.

Homemade: Purchase one small box of macaroni noodles 8 oz size, 3 cups shredded cheddar cheese (mild or sharp from the dairy section), 1 egg, 1 small can carnation or pet milk (baking aisle), soy sauce and 1 8" x 8" aluminum pan. Follow directions on the box for macaroni noodles. Once rinsed and drained, spray bottom of aluminum pan with oil spray, and put ½ of the noodles in the bottom of the pan, add 5 slices of butter at each corner and one in the middle, sprinkle with salt, pepper, garlic and onion powder, top with 1 to 1½ cups of cheese. Add the remainder of the noodles, butter, seasoning etc, but this time, put the butter along the middle of the sides of the pan and also in the middle. Top with remaining cheese (1 to1 ½ cups). In a cup or bowl, scramble one egg, then add ¾ cup canned milk, and 1 to 2 tablespoons of soy sauce with a little salt, pepper, garlic and onion powder and stir. Pour over the macaroni and cheese and bake for 35 to 45 minutes at 350 degrees.

**Dessert:** Buy a variety of fresh fruit from the produce section and make your own fruit bowl or purchase one already prepared. Serve with fruit flavored yogurt or have either one of these as a standalone dessert.

# Dad from a Distance Meal #4:

## Grocery Shopping List

○ Pork Chops – Bone-in or Filet (1 per small child or 1 ½ per teenager/adult)

○ Optional veggie additions to Pork Chop recipe

    ○ 1 Medium Onion

    ○ ½ Green Bell Pepper or

    ○ ½ Red Bell Pepper, or both

○ Steamed Cabbage ingredients

    ○ 1 Medium Onion

    ○ 5 Strips of Bacon *or*

    ○ Package of Salt Pork

○ Optional Veggie – Bag of Frozen Broccoli

○ 1 Container of Frozen Mac and Cheese

  *or* for Homemade Macaroni and Cheese

    ○ 8 oz Box of Macaroni

    ○ 3 Cups Shredded Cheddar Cheese

    ○ Stick of Butter/Margarine

    ○ Soy Sauce

    ○ Eggs

    ○ One 5 oz Can of Evaporated Milk

○ Fresh Fruit and/or Yogurt

○ Optional – Jar Pork Gravy

　　○ **or** Pork Gravy  from Mix

○ 8" x 8" Aluminum

# Dad from a Distance Meal #5:

Baked Chicken

Seasoned Rice

Green Beans or Broccoli

Iced tea, Crystal Light, Milk or water

Cupcakes

## Preparation Instructions:

**Baked Chicken** – Purchase drumsticks (or thighs/wings, etc) from the meat department. Season with salt, pepper, garlic and onion powder (as an option, add a little soy sauce and hot sauce to the chicken). Place in a baking dish or purchased aluminum pan in a 425 degree pre-heated oven for 20 to 25 minutes, remove from oven, turn chicken over and bake an additional 20 minutes. If you are so inclined, spread on a little BBQ sauce, turn up the heat to broil and place chicken under the broiler for about 5 minutes on each side.

Option: Purchase pre-cooked baked or rotisserie chicken from the deli.

**Seasoned Rice** – Purchase either boxed Rice-a-Roni, (which come in a variety of flavors) and follow instructions, or buy an instant microwave ready variety of rice and follow the microwave instructions. Kids usually love yellow rice, which can be purchased and made from scratch by following the package directions.

**Green Beans or Broccoli** – purchase green beans and/or broccoli in the frozen food section and follow the cooking directions on the package. Or purchase canned green beans, drain the liquid and add ½ cup of water or chicken stock, minced garlic, with salt, pepper, garlic, and onion powder in small saucepan over medium heat.

**Dessert:** Purchase cupcakes from the bakery or, if you are adventurous, buy a standard cake mix and pre-packaged frosting and follow the directions on the package. You will need a cup cake pan and cup cake liners as well to complete this task.

# Dad from a Distance Meal #5:

## Grocery Shopping List

- ○ Rotisserie Chicken from the Deli

  *or* for Homemade Baked Chicken

  - ○ Chicken Drumsticks, Thighs, and/or Wings (1 to 2 pieces per person)
  - ○ Soy Sauce
  - ○ Hot Sauce

- ○ 9" x 13" Aluminum Pan
- ○ Rice-a Roni *or* Instant Microwaveable Flavored Rice *or* 1 package of Yellow Rice
- ○ Canned or Frozen Green Beans *or* Frozen Broccoli
- ○ Bakery Cupcakes

  *or* for Homemade Cupcakes

  - ○ 1 Box Cake Mix (Yellow, White, or Chocolate)
  - ○ Eggs
  - ○ Vegetable Oil
  - ○ 1 Container of Frosting
  - ○ Metal Cupcake Pan
  - ○ Paper Baking Cups

# Dad from a Distance Meal #6:

Tacos

Spanish Rice

Iced tea, Crystal Light, Milk or water

Apple Pie a la Mode

## Preparation Instructions:

**Tacos** – Purchase ground beef or ground turkey or chicken breasts, strips or cutlets from the meat section. You will also need lettuce and tomato from the produce section and shredded cheese from the dairy section. Taco shells will be located on the ethnic food aisle along with a package of dry taco seasoning mix. In addition, you will need either taco sauce and/or a salsa depending on your preference.

In a frying pan on medium to medium high heat, brown seasoned (salt, pepper, garlic and onion powder) ground beef or ground turkey and add dry taco seasoning and follow package directions. Chicken can also be used by cutting into bite sized strips, season and follow same directions as above.

Shred or chop lettuce, chop tomatoes and put in individual bowls/containers with a separate bowl for the cheese (some grocers sell pre-shredded lettuce for tacos). Make an assembly line and let the taco making begin. Top with taco sauce and/or salsa.

Hint: You may want to purchase the Taco kit in a box, which will have the shells and sauces included.

**Spanish Rice** – Purchase either instant Uncle Ben's or Rice-A-Roni Spanish rice and prepare as directed.

**Dessert:** Purchase an apple pie (or if you prefer, peach, or blueberry, etc.) from either the deli section already cooked or from the frozen food aisle and follow directions. Top with vanilla ice cream.

# Dad from a Distance Meal #6:

## Grocery Shopping List

- ○ 1lb of meat (Ground Beef, Ground Turkey or Chicken Breast Strips/Cutlets)

- ○ 1 Head of Iceberg Lettuce *or* a Pre-packaged bag of Shredded Lettuce

- ○ 1 to 2 Medium Size Tomatoes

- ○ 1 Package of Shredded Taco/Mexican Cheese

- ○ Taco Shells (Soft or Hard)

- ○ Taco Sauce and/or Salsa

- ○ 1 Box of Instant Microwaveable Rice *or* Box of Spanish Rice

- ○ Pre-Cooked Pie from the Deli *or* Frozen Pie from the Freezer Section

- ○ Optional – Vanilla Ice Cream

# Dad from a Distance Meal #7:

Pizza

Salad

Iced tea, Crystal Light, Milk or water

Brownies

## Preparation Instructions:

**Pizza** – Purchase a frozen pizza with your choice of kid friendly toppings and follow the baking directions or call Pizza Hut, Little Caesar's, Domino's, etc.

If you are lucky enough to have a great pizza place that sells pizza by the slice, go for it.

**Salad** – Pick up a salad in the bag already prepared from the produce section, and a bottle of salad dressing.

**Dessert** – The deli/bakery section may have premade brownies that you can just pick up. If not stop by the baking aisle and buy a box mix and follow the instructions. You will typically need vegetable oil, water and eggs along with an aluminum pan for baking. Follow the directions for making "cake like" brownies, which are a real winner with the kids.

# Dad from a Distance Meal #7:

## Grocery Shopping List

- ○ Frozen Pizza **or** Pizza from your Favorite Local Pizza Place

- ○ Prepared Salad in a Bag,

  *or* for Homemade Salad

  - ○ Lettuce
  - ○ Tomato
  - ○ Shredded Carrots
  - ○ Cucumbers

- ○ Salad Dressing of choice

- ○ Pre-Made Brownies

  *or* for Homemade Brownies

  - ○ 1 Box of Brownie Mix
  - ○ Vegetable Oil
  - ○ Eggs
  - ○ 8" x 8" Aluminum Baking Pan

# Dad from a Distance Meal #8:

Meatloaf

Mashed Potatoes and Gravy

Corn

Iced tea, Crystal Light, Milk or water

Cookies

## Preparation Instructions:

**Meatloaf** – Stouffer's has a great meatloaf and gravy meal that can be popped in the oven or microwave.  If you are making meatloaf from scratch:  Locate a meatloaf-seasoning packet on the seasoning aisle and follow the directions provided. This will provide you with the seasonings and meat quantities and easy directions that can be followed. You will need to purchase an aluminum loaf pan in which to bake the meatloaf.

**Mashed Potatoes and Gravy** – Purchase whole potatoes in the produce section individually or in 5 or 10 pound bags.  Peel potatoes (average of 1 per person) and cut into ½" to 1" cubes. Place in boiling water with 1 teaspoon of salt. Boil potatoes for approximately 20–30 minutes or until soft – test for doneness with a fork. Drain water off potatoes and mash with a fork or potato masher. They don't have to be fully mashed – a few lumps make for good eating. Add 1 tablespoon of butter and ½ cup of milk or half and half (located in the dairy section). The amount of butter and milk you add is in proportion to the number of potatoes being cooked. Add salt and pepper and stir until the potatoes are the consistency desired adding more milk as needed. Sour cream can also be added for additional flavoring.

Use the gravy from the Stouffer's meatloaf or purchase a dry packet of brown gravy mix and follow directions.

Mashed potatoes can also be found in the dairy section or you can use instant mashed potatoes.

**Corn** – Purchase frozen corn from the freezer section and follow directions or use canned corn, drain the liquid and add a tablespoon of butter and ½ cup of water, a little salt and pepper in a saucepan and heat over medium heat for 10 minutes.

**Dessert:** Purchase premade cookies from the bakery/deli section or pick up Pillsbury slice and bake cookies that you can make together with your child. You will need a cookie sheet when making the slice and bake cookies.

# Dad from a Distance Meal #8:
## Grocery Shopping List

○ Stouffer's Meat Loaf and Gravy

   *or* for Homemade Meatloaf

      ○ 1 to 2 lbs of Ground Beef (you can substitute 1 lb of Ground Beef and 1 lb of Ground Turkey)

      ○ 1 Meat Loaf Seasoning Packet,

      ○ 1 Aluminum Loaf Pan,

      ○ Jar of Brown Gravy (or packet of Brown Gravy Mix)

○ Dairy Mashed Potatoes *or* Instant Mashed Potatoes

   *or* for Homemade Mashed Potatoes

      ○ 1 potato per person

      ○ Milk or Half and Half,

      ○ Butter/Margarine

○ Frozen Corn *or* Canned Corn

○ Bakery Cookies *or* Pillsbury Slice and Bake Cookies and Cookie Sheet

# Dad from a Distance Meal #9:

Hot Dogs/Hamburger or Turkey Burger

Baked Beans

Cole slaw/Potato salad

Potato Chips

Iced tea, Crystal Light, Milk or water

Applesauce

**Preparation Instructions:**

**Hotdogs** – Purchase hotdogs from the deli/sandwich meat section. Hotdogs can be boiled in water for about 5 minutes or can be placed in the microwave oven for 30–40 seconds (make sure to pierce them with a fork prior to microwaving). They can also be placed in the oven or toaster oven for 20 minutes. Or fire up the grill and let your true culinary skills shine.

**Hamburgers/Turkey Burgers** – Purchase these from the meat or frozen food section. I would recommend the frozen variety and follow the instructions for proper preparation.

Or, if you prefer, throw them on the grill for that true smoky flavor.

Don't forget the buns and condiments: ketchup, mustard, relish, onion, lettuce, tomato, cheese, pickles and chips.

**Baked Beans** – Purchase Van Camps pork and beans 30 oz size (or any brand of pork and beans) from the canned goods aisle. Place beans in an 8" x 8" aluminum pan, and add a little salt, pepper, garlic and onion powder. Add 1–2 tablespoons of ketchup and 1 teaspoon of mustard. Add ¼ to ½ cup of light brown sugar and 1–2 tablespoons of sugar.  Stir all ingredients together. Bake in a 350-degree oven for 30–45 minutes.

Optional: For additional seasonings and flavor add ½ cup each of chopped onion and green pepper.

If you are in a hurry, you can usually purchase premade baked beans in your grocer's deli section.

**Cole Slaw / Potato Salad** – I would recommend that this be purchased in the appropriate size container from the deli section.

Dessert:  Applesauce (how easy is that!)

# Dad from a Distance Meal #9:

## Grocery Shopping List

- ○ Hot Dogs *or* Frozen Hamburgers *or* Frozen Turkey Burgers

- ○ Hot Dog Buns *or* Hamburger Buns

- ○ Ketchup

- ○ Mustard

- ○ Relish

- ○ Mayonnaise

  For Burgers

  - ○ 1 Head of Lettuce,

  - ○ 1 to 2 Tomatoes,

  - ○ 1 Medium Onion

- ○ Pre-Made Deli Baked Beans

  *or* for Homemade Baked Beans

  - ○ 28–30 oz can of Pork and Beans

  - ○ Sugar

  - ○ Brown Sugar

  - ○ Optional – 1 Onion and 1 Green Pepper

  - ○ 8" x 8" Aluminum Pan

- ○ Deli Pre-Made Coleslaw *or* Potato Salad

- ○ Your Choice of Chips

- ○ 1 Jar of Apple Sauce *or* individual serve packs of Apple Sauce

# Dad from a Distance Meal # 10:

Chicken or Beef Stir Fry

Fried Rice

Iced tea, Crystal Light, Milk or water

Ice Cream Sundae

## Preparation Instructions:

**Chicken or Beef Stir Fry** – There are a variety of frozen stir fry options that either include the meat or only require you to add the chicken or beef which can be purchased in the meat section. I recommend Green Giant or Contessa, but there are several brands from which you can choose.

If you are looking for something that is a little more challenging, I would recommend Sun Bird Beef with Broccoli dry package mix that can be found on the ethnic aisle. Read the package for a complete list of ingredients, but in general this requires beef strips, which can be found in the meat section already cut up, or use a round steak and slice into strips. Purchase frozen broccoli in the frozen section and an onion from the produce section for the ingredients required. Don't forget the soy sauce.

**Fried Rice** – This too can be purchased frozen from freezer section, but for a greater challenge try the Sun Bird Fried Rice dry package mix that can be made with or without meat. Read the package for complete ingredients, but you will need cooked rice (instant will do), scallion/green onion, eggs, soy sauce and frozen peas or peas and carrots. Follow the package directions for a delicious dish.

The vegetable servings will be included with the stir-fry and/or fried rice so you don't have to worry about the veggies.

**Dessert:** Ice Cream Sundae – One scoop of ice cream topped with chocolate syrup, cherries, nuts, whipped cream, coconut, sprinkles etc.

# Dad from a Distance Meal #10:

## Grocery Shopping List

○ Frozen Stir Fry Meal

   *or* for Homemade Stir Fry

   - ○ 1 Stir Fry Seasoning Package (i.e. Sunbird Beef w/ Broccoli)

   - ○ 12 oz Package of Frozen Broccoli

   - ○ 1 Medium Onion

   - ○ Soy Sauce

○ Instant Microwaveable Fried Rice

   *or* for Homemade Fried Rice

   - ○ 2 Cups of Instant Rice

   - ○ 1 Fried Rice Seasoning Package

   - ○ 1 Egg

   - ○ 1 package of frozen Peas & Rice

   - ○ 1 Bunch of Scallions

○ Ice Cream of Choice

○ Chocolate Syrup

○ Jar of Cherries

○ Chopped Nuts of your Choice

○ Whipped Cream

# Your Legacy

# Dad from a Distance

## Your Legacy

After all is said and done, the real measure of what kind of Dad you have been will not be for you to decide; the real measure will be what kind of Dad your children feel you've been to them.

You should, however, have a vision of what you want that legacy to be, and toward that end, I'd like you to take part in a legacy exercise.

In preparation for the exercise, you'll need to:

1.  Get a copy of your favorite picture of each of your children and sit it/them before you.
2.  Get a few pieces of paper to write on, or if you prefer, get prepared to type what's coming up next into a working document on your computer.

Now, I want you to do some visualization.

Project yourself into the future to a time after you're long gone.

And let's say that you'd lived your life as the best possible Dad you could be. That you gave your heart and soul to the effort, with no regrets, and that you'd forged exactly the kind of wonderful relationship with your child that you always wanted, leaving no stone unturned.

Now picture a time when your child is seated in their own home one lazy afternoon, with **their** grandchildren seated at their feet, when one of their grandchildren asks, "What was Great-Grandpa like?"

If you lived your life as a Dad exactly as you'd hoped and dreamed, I want you to actually write down or type what your child would say about you as they reflected back on their relationship with you.

Note: It's important that you just don't think through this exercise, but that you **actually write or type** what you think your child would tell their grandchildren about you in each of these important aspects of your relationship. Do the same exercise for **each** of your children.

**What would your child tell their grandchildren about...**

How you made them feel loved?

How you were always there for them?

How you supported them in their activities?

How you supported their efforts in education?

What you taught them about being responsible with money?

How you encouraged them when they were having a difficult time?

What little things you did to make them feel special?

What you taught them about what a great Dad is really like?

If in this legacy exercise, you liked what your children said about you as a Dad, the question for here and now is "What do you need to start doing now to make creating that legacy today?" or more simply...
"Now what?"

# Now What?

✦

# Dad from a Distance

## Now what?

To start creating the legacy you visualized, it's time to put together a game plan.

There's an old riddle that goes like this:

Question: What's the best way to eat an elephant?
Answer: One forkful at a time.

That's the approach I'm suggesting that you take to create, sustain, and build upon a great ongoing relationship with your child.

It's nothing you should try to, or quite frankly you can do, all at once.

It's about consistently doing the little things that make a big difference over the course of your lives.

My guess is that as you read through some of the "Things to Do" that were outlined in this book, some of them struck you as things that you might like to give a try.

Well to make all this work it's time I suggest that you actually put together a plan by scheduling some of those "Things to Do".

Start by getting a calendar, or using the calendar on your phone or your computer.

Then, actually pick a series of things to do over the next month (one forkful at a time, remember?).

Some "Things to Do", require you to be physically spending time with your child, but many do not. So mix it up.

You don't want all your efforts to be all one or the other, but rather a blend of both.

Here's a local "Dad from a Distance", with visitation every other weekend, plan example:

# Week 1

### Monday

Mail a greeting card that says you're thinking of them, and then send a text message to let them to know to expect something in the mail.

### Wednesday

Attend parent/teacher conference

# Week 2 (visitation weekend)

### Tuesday

Send a postcard

### Thursday

Have a short SKYPE session to find out what's going on this week in their life

### Friday

Movie night at home

### Saturday

Go on a picnic

### Sunday

Cook or go to brunch together

# Week 3

### Tuesday

Take them to 10:00am Dentist appointment

**Thursday**

Text just to say hello

# Week 4 (visitation weekend)

### Monday

Send a text to see what movie they'd like to go see this weekend

### Wednesday

Help them study for their test on Thursday over the phone

### Friday

Taco Night at home

### Saturday

Go see the movie they suggested when you texted them earlier in the week

### Sunday

Call or visit your parents together

If you're a **Long Distance Dad**, meaning you don't live in the same local area as your child or in close proximity, you'll notice that you could probably do a lot of the same things, but obviously, many of these things wouldn't be practical if, say, you lived in another city or state, or even country.

In the case of **Long Distance Dads**, I suggest you rely much more on things like phone calls, texts, e-communication, greeting cards and postcards.

And there a lot of cool things you can do if you focus on being creative.

For example:

1. You can schedule phone calls to each of your child's teachers to discuss how they are doing in their particular classes.
2. You can maintain a dialogue with your child's teachers via e-mail.
3. Many schools have their curriculums on-line, and make grades and progress reports available on-line on the school's website as well. So you can stay in the loop on what and how your child is doing academically via the internet. (Check with your child's school for details)
4. You can do 3-way calls connecting you, your child, and your parents.
5. You can send your child a gift card to their favorite restaurant or even purchase a gift certificate on line to a movie theater in their local area.

With a little effort and some creativity, you'll find that there are numerous possibilities and options to help you stay well connected to your child, even if you are a **Long Distance Dad**.

I also suggest, however, that you plan and budget accordingly to periodically take a trip to your child's hometown.

How often you'll be able to do this, of course, will depend upon your financial situation, but it's a worthwhile investment no matter the cost.

Imagine the look of surprise and joy on your child's face when they look up and see you in the audience at their school play, or in the stands at their ballgame when you live hundreds of miles away.

If you're a **Long Distance Dad**, it'll obviously be more of a challenge for you to sustain a close and meaningful relationship with your child, but it's worth every bit of creativity, energy, and effort you can throw at it.

It's just that important.

# Final Thoughts

# Dad from a Distance

## Final Thoughts

Being a Dad from a Distance obviously comes with a variety of challenges, and the path is no doubt filled with potholes, hurdles, and obstacles of every size and shape imaginable.

It will not be without a significant number of stumbles, mistakes, missteps, and sometimes even heartache.

You will receive tons of advice and counsel from scores of solicited and unsolicited sources; most well intended; some maybe not so much so.

And all of the above will, of course, be the case into the foreseeable future.

Even given all these things, there is no greater gift than having the opportunity to play an integral role in shaping the character and development of your children.

It's about so much more than being a "non-custodial father". That's a title that speaks only to your legal and biological status.

But to be a "Dad from a Distance" - Well, that's a different thing altogether.

To be a "Dad from a Distance" is to have your children know and feel that you love and care about them every moment of every day.

To be a "Dad from a Distance" is to have your children know that you are and will always be there for them in thought and in deed every day of their lives.

To be a "Dad from a Distance" is to show your son the true standard of what a man should really be, and to show your daughter what standard they should measure men by when deciding whom to allow into their lives and be the father of their children someday.

Every father **can** be this type of Dad.

Every father **should** be this type of Dad.

Moms are irreplaceable.

Moms are beautiful.

Moms are wonderful.

Moms are the perfect well source from which we all spring.

It was your child's Mom that gave you the gift of fatherhood.

But being a Dad is pretty special, too.

Just ask any child that has one, or any child that doesn't.

So be one – a **great** Dad, no matter the Distance.

About the Author

Greg Gray is nationally recognized as an authority on leadership, service, and relationship building. He's delivered training and keynote addresses to tens of thousands of people in more than 400 cities across America, Europe, the Caribbean, and the Pacific Rim.

To learn more about Greg, his seminars,
and his programs on DVD,
please visit his website at
www.greggray.com

Join Greg on Facebook
www.facebook.com/greggrayonfb

Made in the USA
Charleston, SC
15 July 2010